The American Holocaust

MARK WROBEL

The American Holocaust

By Mark Wrobel

Cover Created & Designed by Jazzy Kitty Publications

Logo Designs by Andre M. Saunders/Jess Zimmerman

Editor: Anelda L. Attaway

ISBN 978-1-7357874-0-4

Library of Congress Control Number: 2020918467

Jazzy Kitty
PUBLICATIONS

DEDICATIONS

I dedicate this book to two of my favorite teachers for Strayer University; Dr. Cindy Orth and Tom Kasprzak.

ACKNOWLEDGMENTS

First and foremost, I acknowledge God and thank Him for sustaining me through life with my disability.

TABLE OF CONTENTS

INTRODUCTION

I am writing this book to address several issues that the United States citizens should be concerned about. But unfortunately, the American people have become nothing but sheep to the slaughter of the machine that will lead us off the cliff and lead us into the so-called New World order.

By writing this book, I hope to wake up the American people and to open their eyes and let them see what is going on around them in the United States and around the world.

I do not think that this will change anything overnight, especially when the American people have become slaves to the regime that is starting to rule with the iron fist over an entire population.

I do not care what the color of your skin is; I do not care by what name you call God; all I want to do is to give the last warning to humanity before it is too late.

I also feel that I am an American; therefore, I have American responsibilities.

CHAPTER 1

The Beginning of Censorship in America

Everyone in America thinks that the censorship of the media started in 2001 with the passage of the Patriot Act after 9/11; those people could not be more wrong.

The censorship of written material began in the 1950s, and here is how it all started.

After World War II, a lot of those victims of the Holocaust came to the United States. Don't get me wrong; those people did suffer in the concentration camps. If anyone accuses me of being a Holocaust denier, then your wrong, and I do not blame you for that since you have been brainwashed and taught to think with your emotions in our so-called public schools.

With those Holocaust survivors who came to America and a group of people so-called, Judeo Communists started the organization called the Communist Party USA. This organization is responsible for the downfall of America, in my opinion. The Communist Party USA has gain momentum in the 1960s, leading the march against the Vietnam War and leading the charge of the sexual revolution in America, among other things. The Communist Party USA managed, in my opinion, to operate in America quietly until April 19, 1995.

When the Oklahoma City bombing occurred, this is, in my opinion, when the downfall of America and censorship of all media in America began. The censorship has kicked into high gear after the massacre in Columbine High School in Colorado.

Since the so-called Government Educational-Industrial Complex has brainwashed you, I will try to educate you now on how this censorship in America gained momentum after the massacre in Columbine, Colorado. That's correct; the censorship in America kicked into high gear in your local public schools, universities, and colleges, and here is how it works.

After the incident in Colorado, a teacher or a professor can send you to a psychologist or a psychiatrist after they read the papers that you have written. That is correct, ladies and gentlemen; if the teacher does not like what you have written, they can make your life miserable in public schools, and believe me, they have the tools to do it with.

And this is how it started; our so-called Judeo Communist Media has said that one of the gunmen wrote a poem under a title called, "My Best Friend is a Gun" for a class project. In my opinion, writing that type of poem was not a good idea; as a matter-of-fact, I think it was crazy personally. However, the Judeo Communist Media was already crucifying us as writers or anybody who writes an essay on a controversial topic in high school, grade school, or even college.

Here is how the media controlled by Jews can make you into an enemy of the state, not just the media but also your public schools, colleges, and universities.

They can call your parents and say, for example, "Mrs. X, look at what your daughter wrote for a class project. It is too controversial or too violent, and I think we need to put her in the loony bin or on medication, preferably Prozac."

What does Mrs. X. do in that case? Well, she takes her poor daughter home and talks to her husband, Mr. X. (if she has one). I bet you I know how that conversation would go.

Here is a sample, "Hello Honey," says Mrs. X. to her husband after she comes home from the meeting with the teacher, "I spoke with Susie's teacher from the English department at the Communist University. Her teacher told me and showed me what she wrote for a class project. She said that it was too controversial, and she recommended that we put her in the loony bin on the medication Prozac."

After sitting together at dinner, Mr. X. looks at Mrs. X. with his big glasses and a bald head and says to Mrs. X., "You know what, Honey, I think we should put Susie on Prozac as the Prof. Mrs. B. has recommended."

What does an uneducated parent do? By uneducated, I mean a parent who lacks common sense. Don't get me wrong, I like educated people, but some of those so-called educated people lack common sense, that's all.

Today's American people are nothing but sheep because of the lack of knowledge. Just because a college professor or a teacher in a public school tells them something, the poor parents run to the shrink because the professor or teacher tells them to. Look, I understand that you have to have some respect for authority, such as teachers, firefighters, or police officers. However, sometimes you have to question their authority because sometimes those authorities can be wrong; they're only human.

I know that Pres. Eisenhower said, "Beware of the Government Military-Industrial Complex."

I'm about to give you another phrase to memorize, "Beware of the Government Educational-Industrial Complex." Look, those two kids in Colorado messed up their lives, actually ended their lives, and indeed it was a tragic incident. But a reasonable person can still ask, just because those two dummies messed up their lives and everyone else's who was involved in this massacre in Littleton. Does that mean that we all have to face a collective punishment? Because this looks like to me that it's a collective punishment for everyone, the book writers, and students who write controversial papers. They have to watch what they write because if they lean or standout from the crowd, that means they will have to pay the piper.

In America, in my opinion, there is a severe limit on freedom of speech. That's right, ladies and gentlemen, when one person fucks up, we all pay, I think not. If you all want to continue to be the sheep that the government will lead to slaughter, then go right ahead. But I will not go with you or be part of it. I will resist with everything I have left with my mind, body, and spirit. I will not be silent; I will continue my work to make this country better and better. And if you Judeo Bolshevik's think that you will silence me, you picked on the wrong person. One of the reasons I wrote this book is because this is my form of resistance to what is coming in this great country of ours called the United States of America.

CHAPTER 2

Judeo Communist in America and the Media they Own

This chapter will be the most controversial issue that I'm going to address in this book. Who owns the media in the United States of America today? Who is turning the American people into American sheep?

Here is a list of names and what part of the media and corporation they own:

- **Jeffrey Robert Immelt**

  Born on February 19, 1956, he is an American business executive who currently works as a venture partner at New Enterprise Associates. He is most known as becoming the CEO of General Electric on August 1, 2017. He retired from GE as Chairman of the Board on October 2, 2017.

- **Sumner Murray Redstone**

  Born on May 27, 1923, and died August 11, 2020, NBC, MSNBC, CNBC, (birth name Sumner Murray Rothstein). He was an American billionaire businessman and media magnate born in Boston, Massachusetts. He was the majority owner and Chairman of the National Amusements theater chain, the parent company of Paramount Pictures, which includes CBS, BET, and MTV, and MovieTickets.com. He died at the age of 97 in Los Angeles, California.

Can anyone tell me what do those two names above have in common? That's right, ladies and gentlemen, they are Jewish. Some of you will label me as anti-Semitic. Well, I got news for you all you Israel firsters, you anti-Americans, and you so-called Zionist Christians. I am an anti-Semite, and that is my pride. But only for those who spit on my country, the Good Old USA.

Can somebody please tell me why it is okay in America to criticize the Irish (the Polish people), but the Jews get a pass? I think in America, if any ethnic group does anything wrong, they should be criticized for it.

Can anyone explain to me as an American citizen what the benefits of supporting Israel are? In my opinion, you can either be a Christian, Muslim or a Jew; there isn't such a thing as a Judeo Christian. How can we consider Israel as our friend if, in 1967, the Israeli Navy and the Israeli Air Force sank our ship, the USS Liberty, among other things?

Have we as American citizens received any first aid when we had the Katrina disaster in New Orleans from Israel? The answer to that question is NO. And why not? Because ladies and gentlemen, the Zionist state is nothing more than a take-take nation. They do not give anything back in any kind of payment or goods and services. They are nothing more than a welfare check grabber and a slave master to the American people.

The first people to sell themselves like slaves were the Americans by becoming a so-called ally of the state of Israel. Israel is nothing more than a leech on the healthy ass of the United States of America.

My next question is, can someone please explain to me how is that possible that if Israel stops existing, then the United States will cease to exist as well? Look, people, America has existed before 1948, and it will continue to exist.

I think personally that the alliance with Israel by Americans is dangerous for the sovereignty of the United States. I think it would be more beneficial to the United States of America to end its alliance with them. Just look at the gas prices, so I think it would be more beneficial. I think it would be more beneficial to the United States if we had a stronger alliance with the oil-producing nations. It would be even better if we had our own oil production. That way, we would not have to kiss anybody's ass, and we would be more independent and self-sufficient.

CHAPTER 3

Control of the Internet by the Judeo Bolshevik's

You may think that you have freedom of speech on the Internet, and to some degree, that is true. However, I will show you and illustrates to you where freedom of speech is controlled on the Internet.

Let us take a look at a four-minute website called YouTube.

The owner's name of the website YouTube is Mark Zetterberg. There is this gentleman that I will refer to him as Mr. V. for this discussion.

He still has a website called Jew watch that is very popular on the Internet. However, Mr. V. had a very popular video broadcast on YouTube called the Zionist news; mind you, he had this little video blog on YouTube for a long time.

In his videos, he addressed issues of the day without any so-called political correctness or any censorship or bias.

However, there is a certain minority in our country, the United States of America, that did not share Mr. V.'s Political views, so what did they do? They suspended Mr. V.s account from YouTube. By doing that, the Bolsheviks have virtually made it impossible for Mr. V. to have his video blog on YouTube. However, this censorship not only applies to such websites like YouTube, but also it is very prevalent on such sites as Livelink, Myspace, and many others.

Here is my big question for this discussion to all of you, Bolshevik liberals?

I thought that the liberal saying was I may not agree with your views, but I will die for you so that you can say them. In my opinion, however, these people are not the real liberals but Judeo Communist Bolsheviks who will not be happy unless they control everyone all around the world.

Well, guess what you will never control the entire world, whether on the Internet or anywhere else. You will never be able to stop all of the freedom of speech, you communist Bolsheviks you.

Look, you may not agree with Mr. V.'s political views, and you may not agree with anyone else's political views. However, those people still have the protections of the Constitution of the United States in their first amendment of freedom of speech, and that applies to every single American citizen who still believes in the Constitution and the right to free speech.

I know that whatever the Bolsheviks may do, there will always be the right to freedom of speech. Not all people may defend this right; however, the big majority, I hope, will stand up one day.

I hope that by using Mr. V.'s example, I showed you how the Communists Bolsheviks control your speech on the Internet.

CHAPTER 4

One World Government

I've been watching our nation go into decline little by little. As I watched this, I have been trying to figure out who was actually behind this situation, and I concluded that global lists and other entities want this thing to happen, what you may ask?

Well, the one-world government, of course.

You see, the globalists do not want you two to be British, American or Polish or whatever else your nation is. They want you to be easily controlled sheep.

How is this happening, you may ask.

Here is how it works, the United States of America every year loses its sovereignty little by little to the United Nations. You may ask, how is this possible? If the government educational complex monopoly has educated you, you have no idea what I'm talking about. Well, I'm going to educate you from scratch in this case.

In this case, I'm going to give you a brief history lesson.

The United Nations/the UN was created in 1945 at the end of World War II, to prevent future wars; however, this did not work as advertised.

In the late 1950s, the UN has engaged in a war to support South Korea against the North.

In this case, however, this war was totally justified, and the United Nations have acted within its charter to prevent war.

Today, the United Nations is engaging in global governance by dictating how other nations should be run. In this case, the UN is stealing sovereignty from other nations, or the other countries have lost the will to govern themselves.

Here is a dirty little secret that most people do not know someone else is also controlling the United Nations. Here are some groups that control the United Nations, and in turn, they control the whole world. The number one group. The controls the world is the Boulder Berger, the trilateral commission also part of worldwide control. We have in this bunch council on foreign relations and the other controller, and the last controller is the Rothschilds banking Empire.

What you have to understand is that all those people mentioned above do control the entire world.

Those people do not want you to be sovereign citizens of your nations. Whatever the nationality is, they want you to be part of the whole global empire that there building right under your nose.

You may ask yourself this question can this entire global government/New World order be stopped. Yes, it could.

How can we, as people, stop this thing from happening? First and foremost, we have to be very well informed in this war against the New World order guns are not going to be as important as information; armed resistance will be important. It will also be important to have the necessary information on how I think those Judeo Bolsheviks have control?

How do you think they control us by passing treaties, and by signing treaties, the United States is losing its national sovereignty to the United Nations.

Now what they will push for in the United Nations is for the global gun control treaty, and that will band all guns, and the people will not be able to defend themselves or oppose any tyranny that the global elites will throw at them.

Do you think that the American people elect their president of the United States? The answer to that question is most definitely not. That is because the president of the United States is selected by the ruling class mentioned above.

What you have to remember is that you have to as a person to have an open mind and you have to remember is that nothing is what it seems.

Nothing happens without a reason. Everything is part of the plan by the global elites.

CHAPTER 5

Gun Control by the Judeo Bolsheviks

To understand what I'm going to talk about in this chapter, you have to use your brain and have some analytical capability.

When our new President Barack Hussein Obama got elected in 2009, he said that he would band all guns from a private citizen. A private citizen in America could not own a gun to defend himself against the cruel criminal element and the government. In case the government became a tyrant to the people of the United States.

You have to understand that the Second Amendment to our Constitution allows us to own guns not only to go duck hunting and deer hunting but also to protect ourselves against criminals and our government in case it becomes a tyrant.

Ladies and gentlemen, it looks like the Bolsheviks are going at it again, but this time they are doing a very outrageous thing to gun owners of America.

Let us look at the tragedy at Sandy Hawk elementary school in Connecticut.

I am not saying that the school shooting was an inside job. However, this particular incident has all the desirable effects on the liberal gun-control agenda.

You see, the Liberals will never take away our guns if we can help it.

Here is how the new gun controls work. The Bolsheviks cannot take away our guns. However, they still control the availability of ammunition for the guns the ammunition such as 22 Long rifle and some other calibers are, as of this writing is very difficult to get or it is very expensive.

I know what you are thinking, how can a guy like me right about such a topic? That is because I think I still live in a relatively free country, and I can still analyze all kinds of situations.

My wish is that all of the American people did have a good analytical mind, just like me.

If the American people got together and finally had a look inside the Judeo Bolshevik agenda, in my opinion, those Bolsheviks would not have a chance to implement their plan.

CHAPTER 6

The European Union and Who is Behind It

Have you ever wondered how did the European Union got started?

As an average United States citizen, have you ever wondered why does the European Union flag has 12 stars on the blue background on their flag?

In this particular chapter, I will try to answer these questions from my point of view.

The European Union was started back in the 30s by a certain German leader that we all know. However, he tried to implement his plan of the European Union by force. However, we all know how his plan failed back in 1945.

The puppet masters behind the curtain did not give up the idea of a one-world government, which the German leader between 1939 through 1945 tried to implement.

We all know that the European Union got its start, by simple trade agreements, between European nations; at that time, people did not understand what was going on. That is because the puppets behind the curtain did not reveal their plan until it was too late.

Of course, we all know that there European Union was started by Germany and the German industrialists/globalists.

In the future, those European nations will not even have their own language because the language of Esperanto will replace all of the Slavic languages and many others. The language of Esperanto contained a little bit of every language that is spoken in Europe today. This is the simplest way to explain (Wikipedia, 2020).

You see, European Union has its own currency called the euro as well, overtime after they nations give up their sovereignty, unfortunately with trade agreements and other things, if the globalists will have their way, we will have a global currency which they are working on right now.

Have you ever wanted to know why there are 12 stars on the European Union flag?

That is because the European Union has been created by the 12 tribes of Bolsheviks/fascists.

Yes, they even do exist, under the name of Majestic 12 here in America, and yes, George Herbert Bush was privy to, and some speculate that he was, the member of the group of majestic 12.

The majestic 12 did not only deal with UFOs, but they are privy to other secrets as well, especially about the global governance and one-world government. If you want more information about the majestic 12, here is the information. (Wikipedia, 2020)

You might be asking yourself a question right about now. You do not believe in this one-world government, do you?

I would tell you this right now if I met you, about 5 to 10 years ago, I would've said to you that you were out of your mind. However, because of some of my research that I have done, I not only believe that there is a new world order, but I also know that most of our political decisions are not made in our capitals, not any longer.

Even the 1991 speech that was given by former president George Bush has confirmed this idea. (YouTube, 1991).

There is one country in this world, who has stood up to the global elites and said that is enough. We are no longer going to be part of this global governance; that country that has accomplished this is Great Britain/England.

However, after so-called Britain leaving the European Union, the British people have a lot of work to do to regain their sovereignty.

Of course, we have something similar to the European Union here in America, and that is called the North American Union. However, President Donald J. Trump has slowed down the March of the globalists and the North American Union. He has not completely stopped it. The reason is, unfortunately, because he cannot totally stop it, for obvious reasons.

I wrote this book to show you where the problem is and help you survive what is going on now and what has been going to go on in the United States for quite some time. (2020)

ABOUT THE AUTHOR

My name is Mark Wrobel, and I reside in Wilmington, Delaware. I was born with a disability, but I didn't allow that to stop me from excelling in life.

My father raised me; he was a dedicated single parent. I grew up in a communist system. Due to my disability, my country would not allow me to attend school with regular kids, but I persevered.

Fortunately, when about 10-years-old, I came to the United States, which I knew was the land of opportunity. So I took full advantage of it and made sure I got a good education.

From 1989 until 1993, I attended St. Thomas The Apostle School, a Catholic school in Wilmington, Delaware.

Then in 1993, I attended Wilmington High School and graduated in 1997 with a high school diploma.

In 2002, I attended Delaware Tech Community College to attend their Web Designer Certificate Program, which I completed.

I continued my education in 2008 at Strayer University, studying Information Systems and Homeland Security. I graduated from Stayer in 2012 with an Associate Degree.

In 2018, I returned to Strayer University to obtain my Bachelor of Science degree in Information Systems and Homeland Security

Management and graduated in 2020. I am proud of this accomplishment because I was told that it was impossible, and I couldn't do it.

I am currently employed with the United States Coast Guards in Communications. I began working for the Coast Guard in 2012. Thus far, I have received multiple awards and accolades for my dedicated service.

I love to learn and try new things. In 2007, I decided to try sky diving, and with the help of an instructor, I jumped 18,000 feet. There was an article published about it in the News Journal.

In the future, I would still like to go back to school to obtain my master's and a doctoral degree.

I am the author of the title Progressive Credentialism Versus Ageism, which is available online worldwide. This is my second book, and I couldn't have done it without my father's support.

REFERENCES

- Who Owns the Media in the US
  http://en.wikipedia.org/wiki/ Sumner_Redstone
  http://www.bing.com/search?q=jeffrey+immelt+jewish+ms+nbc&
  qs=HS&sk=HS1&pq=je&sc=8-2&sp=2&FORM=QBRE&cvid=
  4fc6d

- Anti-American organizations in the US
  Here is the list of organizations that work with the communist
  party USA against the US.
  http://cpusa.org/
  http://www.nclr.org/

- One World Government
  http://en.wikipedia.org/wiki/World_Bank
  http://en.wikipedia.org/wiki/Bilderberg_Group
  http://www.stopthenorthamericanunion.com/
  http://www.omniglot.com/writing/esperanto.htm
  http://en.wikipedia.org/wiki/Members_of_the_Council_on_Foreig
  n_Relations
  http://www.un.org/en/
  http://www.apfn.org/apfn/fed_reserve.htm
  http://en.wikipedia.org/wiki/Federal_Reserve_Bank

- Attack by Israel on USS liberty

- Attack by Israel on USS libertyhttp://www.gtr5.com/

- Gun Control by Judeo Bolshevik
  http://www.ammoland.com/2013/06/the-united-nations-is-prepping
  -for-global-gun-control/#axzz2s1O9CfpT

- Drugging of the Population by the Judeo Bolshevik Global
  Government and Disarming of the US Population
  http://breggin.com/index.php?option=com_content&task=view&id
  =70&Itemid=99999999

- The Biggest Crime Against the American People by the Judeo
  Bolsheviks/Communists
  https://www.usslibertyveterans.org/

- George Bush his Speech About the New World Order in 1991
  https://www.youtube.com/watch?v=8DtEcZ3cfg4

- The Language of the New World Order
  https://en.wikipedia.org/wiki/Esperanto

- Who are the Majestic 12
  https://en.wikipedia.org/wiki/Majestic_12

- Great Britain Leaving the European Union
  https://www.bbc.com/news/uk-politics-32810887

www.ingramcontent.com/pod-product-compliance
Lightning Source LLC
Chambersburg PA
CBHW062122040426
42336CB00041B/2233